"Poet Adela Najarro's *Variations in Blue* is rich with gratitude for her inheritances despite the suffering which accompanies them. Through poems vibrantly populated by parrots, iguanas, mothers, and abuelitas, it is clear Najarro is a daughter of Nicaragua, with more than a loving nod to 'the gods and goddesses of volcanoes [who] meet up for a barbeque' and her own parents who emigrated to the United States. With her eyes on the 'generations . . . that keep doing the same thing,' the poet at the center of this book is a survivor, aligning herself not only with other women, but also with the heat at the heart of the volcanoes of Nicaragua. In ekphrasis, persona poems, and laments, Najarro's artistry alchemizes that survival and heat into hardearned wisdom which simmers on the page."
—Farnaz Fatemi, author of *Sister Tongue*
    and Poet Laureate of the city of Santa Cruz, 2023–24

"In *Variations in Blue*, Adela Najarro paints pictures of impressionable moments in time, emotional residue that is both hazy and absolute in its confidence, and family tales indomitable in its truth. Her poetry is rich with tales of lost family members and memories pulled from a history of migration and identity. In one poem, Najarro describes La Virgen de las Patadas as having 'hair brown and straight. India, Mexicana, Americana,' cementing the ideas of complexity in Latinx heritage. Yet, throughout this exploration of identity, Najarro always comes back to the landscape, the 'lowest branch of the eucalyptus tree,' the 'scar of the mountain,' and the 'verdant jungle sky,' as if these poems are incantations being witnessed by the glory and violence too of the nature where, 'hombres, mujeres, the gendered not, speak the world.' Here is a book that requires a reader to witness the 'words and omens as talisman' and listen, each poem bringing forth its own tale and its own form of invocation of self and absolute certainty."
—Nikia Chaney, author of *To Stir &* and founder of Jamii Publishing

"Navigating the intersection of Nicaraguan heritage and American life 'backward in a line / of women before memory and photographs,' Adela Najarro's bilingual collection of poetry, *Variations in Blue*, is a deep well of memory.

These poems are sensory, vivid depictions of biodiversity—a country filled with mango trees, freshwater sharks—set against cultural and political turmoil. Ultimately, grounded by heritage and ancestry, *Variations in Blue* delivers a voice both intimate and resilient."

    —Ruben Quesada, author of *Brutal Companion*

"Poet Adela Najarro brings us in full display an identity affirmation and a mature poetic quest in *Variations in Blue*. Her 'todo se confunde' Spanish translanguaging brings a sumptuous collage of what it really means to be a Latin American woman poet, 100% of each: 'Where'd the green eyes come from?' and 'Latin America. The history. / My eyes from los conquistadores / from collison / and struggle / to survive.'

    This poetry collection is a meta history of Central America, from colonization, religion, exploitation, to the present state of life for Latines in the United States: 'To avoid offending Padre nuestro, on Fridays / during Lent iguana stew is ladled over rice.'

    Among desires for mangos and Coca Cola, 'aphrodisiac iguanas,' and all the Central American countries, we find the purity of the strongest arrangements of poignant, familiar words turned to poetry in the hands of Adela Najarro—a master wordsmith: 'with a squirrel / in one limb and an iguana in another.'

    Metaphors of her American and Latina self emerge throughout the collection, embracing Chicanos and Nicaraguans alike, as well as all other Latines. Also, her keen eye brings Chicane/Latine art to life in her poetic narrative that raises paintings that have not perhaps been celebrated as they should be.

    Her narrative poems about painters are a levantamuertos, bringing to the public eye, through her words, the colors and interests of Latine sensitivities, and immortality of these pieces, from Esther Hernandez to world-renowned Georgia O'Keefe: 'Be grateful. You have found / cool water in the desert while sipping / from a glass of stones.'"

    —Gabriella Gutiérrez y Muhs, Professor: Modern Languages /
        Women, Gender and Sexuality Studies, Seattle University and
        author of *¿How Many Indians Can We Be? / ¿cuántos indios podemos ser?*

Variations in Blue

poems

ADELA NAJARRO

Red Hen Press | *Pasadena, CA*

Book layout by Mark E. Cull

Library of Congress Cataloging-in-Publication Data

Names: Najarro, Adela, author.
Title: Variations in blue: poems / Adela Najarro.
Identifiers: LCCN 2024034968 (print) | LCCN 2024034969 (ebook) | ISBN
   9781636282749 (paperback) | ISBN 9781636282756 (ebook)
Subjects: LCGFT: Poetry.
Classification: LCC PS3614.A5729 V37 2025 (print) | LCC PS3614.A5729
   (ebook) | DDC 811/.6—dc23/eng/20240806
LC record available at https://lccn.loc.gov/2024034968
LC ebook record available at https://lccn.loc.gov/2024034969

Publication of this book has been made possible in part through the generous financial support of Letras Latinas program sponsor James Wilson.

The National Endowment for the Arts, the Los Angeles County Arts Commission, the Ahmanson Foundation, the Dwight Stuart Youth Fund, the Max Factor Family Foundation, the Pasadena Tournament of Roses Foundation, the Pasadena Arts & Culture Commission and the City of Pasadena Cultural Affairs Division, the City of Los Angeles Department of Cultural Affairs, the Audrey & Sydney Irmas Charitable Foundation, the Meta & George Rosenberg Foundation, the Albert and Elaine Borchard Foundation, the Adams Family Foundation, Amazon Literary Partnership, the Sam Francis Foundation, and the Mara W. Breech Foundation partially support Red Hen Press.

    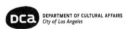

 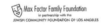

First Edition
Published by Red Hen Press
www.redhen.org

For Juanita Pinell, Epple, Ouellette, my mother,
whose enduring love fortifies my bones and who birthed me
through Nicaragua's volcanic waters.

You taught me not to fear fire but to embrace
the flames of our turbulent lives.

Contents

II

III

Variations in Blue

I

Remember . . . remember was now the theme
of all our conversations . . .

—Julia Alvarez
from "Last Night at Tías"

Again, Nicaragua

This time, we picnic by a river. The river is smooth.
The water is clear. There are mangoes in a basket.
I try to focus and freeze the frame. Instead, I float

downstream. Again, Nicaragua, but the crocodiles
are missing. There are no iguanas. Just the river. The water.
At journey's end, a homestead. The family.

They are not my family. They're American tourists.
White with grandpa. We climb up a sea cliff trail
as waves rush and gurgle round lava stone.

Pathways up. The Americans leap over crevices with fine
smooth muscle. I follow. Grandpa tells me not to.
He is tired and wants a Coca-Cola.

I reach the top, anyway. At the homestead,
I show an old movie where Somoza waltzes Mamie
at Camp David. It's part of a National Geographic special

about monkeys lost in space and brown people jailed
down South. Deviled eggs curdle in humidity and heat.
Again, I dream about this house, this home, ancestors

at the top of a sea cliff. Shore breezes and palm trees.
Birds of paradise. A handwritten note
on fine linen stationery. A picture on the back.

An oval frame. Bald. Suit. Collared shirt. A thin tie.
This is my great-grandfather. El brujo.
The one who cures malaria with fine powders

while casting out susto. He resembles
my Tío Francisco and my brother.
That oval European skull. Even though

sepia, the hazy yellow of past times, it is
obvious. He is white. Genteel. Master of all
he commands. The river. The water. We float.

Poneloya Poolside Party

We're vacationing at a resort. All the apartment tiers have lower decks with infinity pools pouring into the ocean. My mother says we know the people who live here and knocks on a door. A silver-haired gentleman in a white suit smiles an invitation. He pauses, then recognizes my mother, ¡*Juanita!* He invites her to jump into the pool, but instead she climbs over the fence and disappears. I ask him for directions. I want to know the way out. He tells me there are stairs. The stairs lead to the sea. I swim around boulders and over waves to the next bay. Now I'm with my father's family, with my grandmother, my Lela, after whom I am named. We go have lunch downtown where the plaster white plaza curves into a restaurant made from an old yacht. My cousins have oysters and prawns in butter sauce. They laugh and discuss where to buy a new pair of jeans. I return poolside. My mother is there talking with Tía Teresa. I begin to cry because this is just like she told me. Girls in bikinis play volleyball in the pool. Old ladies crochet lace doilies under patio umbrellas. There is laughter. Music rises to a cloudless sky. Whiskey glasses clink.

Iguana Dreams

Before coming to the United States,
Miguel went in pursuit
of the common green iguana.
It was Nicaragua. He was riding a jeep
with friends who carried rifles.

Moving faster than cars idling
at the Tex-Mex border,
the desert iguana scurries through shadow,
brings on the sun.

Highly adaptive, iguanas swim
in the sea and slide through deserts.

For over 7,000 years iguanas
have imbued potency and healed
the weary. Crushed into a paste,
she is also an aphrodisiac.

Iguana power. Iguana dreams. Green scales
glisten wet throughout Nicaragua. The rivers,
arboreal forests, humid sky, all percolate water.

Where the scars rise on my right ear,
I dreamed of placing an iguana tattoo.

Iguana meat can be broiled, sautéed,
or fried. Miguel said he made iguana
stew, then promptly got ill.
Something about the unforeseen
brewing at high temperatures.

In Mexico, Guatemala, Belize, El Salvador,
Honduras, Nicaragua, Costa Rica, Panama,
she digs deep to bury her eggs.

To avoid offending Padre nuestro, on Fridays
during Lent iguana stew is ladled over rice.

The morning Tía Teresa saw la guardia
drive up and Miguel ran, an iguana witnessed
all, perched on a cement block wall.

After an earthquake shattered
living room walls, and they were never
rebuilt, Miguel shot the iguana.
Then he came to the United States.

Somewhere in Texas or Arizona,
there might be one lone tree, a grand
old crotchety oak, with a squirrel
in one limb and an iguana in another.

Mujeres

Yo soy Adelita the third, the third
Adela in a backward line
of women before memory and photographs:
Mitadela or Tía Pinita rocking away
a hot afternoon in León, or it could be Managua.
I don't know. Todo se confunde.

It's not only me. We all contribute
to erasure. ¿Qué han hecho las mujeres,
las latinas, mejicanas, dominicanas,
puertorriqueñas, y si también las nicaragüenses?
Todas ocultadas in this US
culture, in this version of history,
in these times of economic chaotic splendor.

To forget your mother's birthday
is to be una gran hija mala,
but of course I must take note
de todas esas mujeres de mi vida y del pasado.
Una después de otra contribuyendo,
haciendo tanto, criando nuestras penas,
curando nuestras heridas, amándonos
por el resto de nuestras vidas.

I carry many names as daughter,
la hija de Juanita, Lela, Mitadela, y Tía Pinita.
A daughter de todas las planchadoras,
lavanderas, maestras y damas de casa
watching telenovelas on Univision wondering
if María Dolores will ever be found
hiding in a convent.

Does being a woman have to entail
una vida de sufrimiento?

I try to swing out from the shadows,
touch the lowest branch
of a eucalyptus tree, and over the years
have found words at rest in mi pasado y las voces
de las poetas olvidadas
sin recompensación, pero todavía vivas,
the women, the mothers
alive in our hearts.

We look to the East
cada mañana y hambriente
para el sol
comienza la aurora.
The women, their words,
their stories
ascend into the morning sky.

Idiomas Desconocidos

The scar of the mountain is as beautiful as the mountain.
The withered branch of the tree bends gracefully to tierra.
Desert earth puts forth one miniature orange flower.
There is softness in the green broken burr.
And still what captures most are leaves lifting
as wind sopla en idiomas desconocidos.

What Comes Back While Standing at the Museum
   Viewing Rafael Soriano's *Un Lugar Distante*
   (*A Distant Place*), 1972, Oil on Canvas

It would have been fall. Before Halloween
and Thanksgiving. Tío Ernesto

painted in the garage. There were magazines,
boxes, tools, and brushes.

A TV tuned to a football game.
I had read *The Martian Chronicles* and thought

of settling on Mars. I would roll
over red rock canyons in a dune buggy.

My tío painted geometric
abstractions. His reality flat, straight,

and pure. He held my hands,
spun me around,

the petals of my skirt
twirling through afternoon.

Tío Ernesto cooked homemade stews
for his perritas and would whistle

for us primos to come running through K-Mart.
My tío and Mars.

Mars and my little girl brain.
An empty red planet filled

with ghosts. Martians who turned into Jesus.
Martians who bounced

as golden spheres of light. Martians
who were no longer afraid. They had returned

to stardust. My tío sang his own body.
There were home movies. Birthday parties. Christmas.

El rojo. Tío Ernesto's more-than friend. His probable
amante hidden behind bags of groceries and a smile.

In one film, there's a parade. Tío Ernesto
runs from one float to the next.

Finally, he climbs up and kisses the beauty
pageant queen. She crowns him with her tiara.

All glitters in 16 mm
as my tío waves and blows kisses.

From the Neighborhood

—upon viewing Jesse Treviño's *Mis Hermanos*, 1976, acrylic on canvas

Have you seen
Treviño's hermanos?
A portrait
de los seis
sitting on a fence.
El chiquito,
plastic cup
in hand. Otro con
mis tío's sunglasses.
I see Guillermo
y Esteban. El Guapito
lifts his chin
and we all know
the trouble
he's been in.
Then Beto with wine.
The fine suede shoes
and trouser socks.
Center straight up
is the one who
will be Papí,
somebody's dad,
her darling
husband. The one
who works, sweats,
and pays the bills,
even after
his preciosa
muchachita
stays out
one night
too late
and her dancing
ends up
as trouble.

La Virgen de las Patadas

—upon viewing Ester Hernandez' *La Virgen de Guadalupe defendiendo
los derechos de los Xicanos*, 1975, etching and aquatint

She kicks the moon in black and white,
a karate side snap paired with a power punch.

Her legs strong and powerful. Her hair
brown and straight. India, Mexicana, Americana,

at the US–Mexico border. La Virgen de las Patadas,
a powerhouse for women caught underneath

bridges, for men resting in blue palo verde shade,
for boys in mismatched tennis shoes. One tattered

bra left roadside. One pair of jeans discarded.
A sun faded box of Gamesa saltine crackers

and an empty plastic jug next to stones
bleached dry. A lizard. Too much sun.

An archangel of the Americas, un luchador
ready to pounce, holds up a golden crescent

y la virgen. For a prayer y una ofrenda,
she'll shoot a frozen star across night sky.

With her blessing, todo estará bien.
You've reached the other side.

La Tempestad

—upon viewing Arturo Rodríguez's, Sin Título,
     from the series La Tempestad, 1998, oil on canvas

As Dorothy speaks Spanglish in Kansas,
her neck spirals past barns,
chicken coops, and soybean fields.

A cultural migration, but she doesn't
go it alone. Un m'ijo holds onto a kite.
Another boy wears a homespun mask.

Autumn light fades fast. He raises
his hands, not wanting any trouble.
Boohoo. This is not a hold up.
I don't want your money.

Dorothy's thin body turns some more
as one handmade corn tortilla
browns in a skillet. She can't get back
since she is Dora, Dorita, facing nowhere,
nothing. She traded her ruby slippers
so los coyotes would leave her body alone.

Her head hangs low. She is downcast
and off-center. Tree branches frame an ancient
face of the Americas. Her body, frail, emaciated.

She holds a root in her palm.
Inside her fingers clenched tight,
the power to bear fruit.

If only she can change
una curandera into a good witch
and click her heels three times.

On Viewing Gronk's *Illegal Landscape* / *Paisaje Ilegal*

Gronk's three panels

splatter

the browning of America
from ceiling to floor.

The view remains
undetermined.

On which side of the border?

Corn grows in suburban backyards.

A woman's clavicle,
beautiful in every color.

Gronk's fence is rusted,
a double string of barbed wire
anchored at the bottom

of the painting.

The fence tears blue tongues,

snags
Chiclet teeth,
cracks open
a Molotov cocktail.

Such violence.
Boom. Explosion.

Chocolate ice cream melts.

A designer handbag
crumbles onto a pile
of cement bricks.

Jaguar paw prints
saunter past

swimming pool
reflections.

Delicate fingers pick at fine silks.

The cone is a volcano. El volcán,

an Aztec warrior. The warrior
points toward a city landscape,

after safe passage:
cement, glass, asphalt.

An Ambiguity

Until syllables undulate a Nicaraguan cadence,
I am a white girl. Once I was asked,

"Where'd the green eyes come from?"
The question arising from longing for a simple

explanation: a gringo father and a love story
where Lupita throws down a rose. Un amorcito

mío once told me not to worry because I was
brown inside. Even so, for a while I dyed my hair

almost black. I still wear gold hoop earrings,
but I haven't tattooed that iguana on the inside

of my right wrist. Her Honorableness Sotomayor
got rid of the subdued hues and laid on

red nail polish after her confirmation. She began
the business of being herself. My mother

keeps insisting that I was born blond. Blondness.
Whiteness. I have been so confused.

I look in the mirror y quiero un color quemado.
A burnt umber. La pimienta. The prickly spice

of tropical brown. But I am güera, chele, fair-skinned,
blanquita. Desde América Latina.

Latin America. The history.
My eyes from los conquistadores.

From collision

and a struggle

to survive.

April in Pico Rivera

It all came clear under a blue dust
sky after a haircut. I was nearly seven.

We lived close, right next door to Nena,
Quique, Tío Enrique y Tía Marelena.

We made a conga line on roller skates.
Rolled over concrete driveways. Nena

was queen. We did what we were told.
Exiting the flea market, we stopped.

I got a beagle. He kept turning circles,
yapping happiness. *You're crazy,*

I said as he jumped into my arms.
I let his smelly dog tongue lick my face.

I wanted something of my own.
Distinction. Difference. A definitely

mine. His belly was tight as a drum.
He had black spots. I didn't know

how to describe a whirling dervish
singular puppy. He was unusual. He came

when I called. He loved me more.
Especially then. I was angry,

heartbroken. My father silent on the phone.
My mother held in so much

as she poured us into a broken down
station wagon. It must have been

difficult to breathe at KFC.
We munched on buttered corn.

I didn't know I would always be trying
to keep holding a hand that wanted

only to let go. Pico Rivera was too hot.
I was sweaty. My puppy

uncontrollable, nonconforming,
unpredictable. He randomly

exhibited excited behavior. With great
speed and recklessness, he entered

the garage. At the back, inside
a musty box with a gnawed corner,

waited a rat's gnarly teeth.

I Didn't Know Much

I went once to Nicaragua where they
soak nancites in water and sugar.
I was thirteen and prepared for heat
with a few pairs of shorts. It was humid
and there were taunts from boys on a bus passing by.
My Tía's house had an inner patio open to sky.
The only way I met neighbors was by climbing
a cement block wall leading up to the roof.
There they were. The boy and the girl
with a monkey on a leash. It was their pet.
I told them I, too, could have been born there,
but they didn't believe me. They thought
I was Americana. Una gringa.
In the evening, it was a little less hot.
The maid, the lady who took care
of everyone and everything, la criada
criando la familia, washed clothes
in the back at an outdoor sink. Maybe
she wasn't doing laundry. They did have
a washing machine. She was there, working.
Her name wasn't said that often. She was a shadow
in the corner. She laughed when I saw
the cockroach. It had wings
and was the size of a big toe.
I was shocked that insects could grow
so large. It buzzed, too. Or are those June bugs
back in the States that get trapped
against screen doors? I didn't know much
about Nicaragua or the US. I was
uncertain, barely a teenager, but I noticed
sidewalks were missing and homes
by the side of the road were coming undone.
Each house, four walls of unpainted cinder blocks.
The windows and doors, open without glass,

without screens, without locks and latches.
There were no sprinklers.
We drove by. All of our family
lived elsewhere.

The History of Food

Maybe in a past life, I was the dairymaid
who after warming her hands on Bessie's udder

dreamed of petticoats, ribbons, and strudel. Maybe
I knocked over the can and spilt the milk on purpose,

angry that the sloshing pail wasn't mine. And since
I didn't get enough milkshakes, I blossomed within a mother

obsessed with soothing children by whirring up milk, butter,
and sugar into fancy éclairs with pastry cream centers.

My mother fed me cream cheese lattes laced with formula
so that my teeth wouldn't bite her nipples. After drinking my fill,

I'd sleep fast under a musical mobile where a cow jumped
over an oatmeal cookie moon. Once to get her attention, I plopped

into the bath wearing a new lace dress, then slurped a hazelnut
milkshake spiced with a peppermint dollop. When cream rises

to the top and becomes cheesecake, little girls fall asleep full
and without crying. My mother knew this. Cream in particular,

such as in cream cheese, cream puffs, slightly sweet tangy
mascarpone whips, soothes the savage little girl beast.

That never happened. My mother never found pleasure
whisking milk, vanilla, and sugar into pudding. On that finca

in Nicaragua, there weren't enough beans to go around and milk
curdled too quickly. She did dream about los Estados Unidos,

pearl necklaces, silk stockings, and big bands playing. Instead,
she found my father. Then, there she was:

in San Francisco with a colicky baby, fog floating past
her plain but sturdy wool coat.

The History of Food II

When mangoes fall to the ground, ants go on parade.
Flies hover. The painted pony down the street gets loose

to spend an afternoon with syrupy sweet on its hairy lips,
slowly sucking one mango seed dry, then onto another.

There are nancites, mamón, jocote, guayaba, aguacate, piña,
mandarina y melón. Bananas and mangoes in refrigerated cargo hulls.

But what about coffee? El café! ¡Oro del corazón! Y coco y cacao.
Australia, India, Polynesia, the Americas. World-wide distribution.

It has always been about not rotting on a ship. Transit.
Crossing borders. The tomato and potato.

So many seeds and eyes sprouting. Seeds dry quickly.
Place them in soil with a bit of water. There you go:

a plant loving the sun. A plant growing fragrantly full.
A plant turning out tomatoes within four months

of warm and balmy afternoons. A sugary explosion
for the mouth. A cultivated gift from the Americas.

And now pizza! In a refrigerator freezer. Tear the cardboard box.
Slice off the plastic wrap. Preheat the oven to 425°.

Eat the whole thing. Then wonder why you're still hungry.

The History of Food III

Holidays used to be holy days when penitentes
would hoist crosses on shoulders to march

around town, a procession. They would fall
to their knees, then grind rocks into skin.

The truly virtuous flayed themselves,
one lash for every thought, deed,

and all they had failed to do. Up, down, and around
endless streets, los penitente's eyes swirled

with the ecstasy of pain, pupils wide
like an owl's hunting a mouse scampering in a field.

Months later, the mouse dead and gone,
a dusty pellet of fur and bones. Not so for el penitente,

roasting green chili for his pork and potato supper.
He knew all had been forgiven, for a while at least.

II

The words are maps.
I came to see the damage that was done
and the treasures that prevail.

—Adrienne Rich
    from "Diving into the Wreck"

The Parking Lot

It was Wednesday or Tuesday. It could have been Thursday around noon
or one o'clock. The sun would have been out or it could have been raining. It
was a day in Southern California. By then the freeways would have begun
to clog or maybe it would have been late enough for them to begin to empty.
Some odd time of day or evening. 2:00 a.m. or 3:46 p.m. or 7:17 p.m. Maybe
it was July. It could have been August. I could have been married. Maybe it
was before we got married. Sometime during the honeymoon. Una luna de
miel. In Spanish, you can hear the moon dripping sweet, sweet, sweetness.
It was the honeymoon. Or you could say the days before we got married
and the days immediately following. The first time we were in a parking lot.
A burger stand off the highway. We needed a walk, so we parked on asphalt
between white lines. Maybe we pulled up and parked off the curb. There
were two burgers wrapped in parchment paper. Cheese melting. Ketchup
in miniature white cups. Two boys crossed the parking lot to their truck.
A yellow pickup with a border collie in the back. That was the first time
he punched my arm. Did I tell you there was a sky? There was a tree, too.
Some grass. He didn't like me looking at the boys. I don't remember the
second time. Nor the third. Every town has a CVS or Walgreens or a
Piggly Wiggly. Stores to buy things we need. The strangest thing is how
did he know? We bought Preparation H and spread the calm on my upper
arm so the bruise would fade. A bruise shaped like California slipping
down into Mexico after an earthquake-shattering fault line. Streets will
flood after the big one comes. Warm rushing water streams in. It did heal
faster, the bruise. The deep congealed bruise: yellow, then green, then
spiraling back to smooth unblemished flesh.

I Have Heard

It is possible that love escapes
only to rise softly from silence,

that daffodils buried underground
stir as shadows retreat,

that a sunset woven into a field of rye
encourages heartache to laugh,

delicately, then robust and full.

Sometimes, a beat-up pickup truck
brings happiness

or it might tell a different story,

one where a collapsed rear fender
and broken tail light are what follow

repetitive lies, too much whiskey, slow
simmered ribs and a sour stomach.

Those risen from the dead
often hear sunflowers turning.

Those who do not rise stay soaked
in rain-filled quagmires.

It is probable that suffering stops,
no matter what.

I have heard that such relief

comes as dervishes spin or during meditation,
prayer, twelve clicks across a rosary.

It is possible for a lilting lemon tree
to absorb laughter rising

from those unable to breathe,
and in so doing,

turn sadness draped down and through
into yellow and seed.

Occasionally, roots from the soles
of our feet spread into soil.

Through our moist and pliable skin,
all runs its course to the end.

Star Variation in Blue

if the world is fracture and uncertainty
        let us take comfort in the unknown
        and pray alongside the meek and humble

rainfall collects then rushes through

        a bend in the river
        a gutter in an alley
        a drain set in concrete

        let us take comfort in the unknown
        and pray alongside the meek and humble

once concentric spheres made the sky

once God wore a beard and sandals

once we were   water   sky   stars

let us take comfort in the unknown
        if the world is fracture and uncertainty

        a bone can fracture
        a body bleed
        that is certain

when a bone fractures
        guttural vowels howl

when a body bleeds
        consonants cannot stop the pain

it is certain that vowels escape

chaotic
hard

into what cannot be written

    as bones fracture
    as bodies bleed

let us take comfort in the unknown
    and pray alongside the meek and humble
the world is fracture and uncertainty

in the beginning
    a woman loved the stars
    a man loved God
    both loved rainfall rushing

through concentric spheres in the sky

it was known the Goddess

    had thick breasts
    belly and thighs

and that we are brought to life
    through   water   sky   stars

let us take comfort

the world

too often

is fracture and unknown

that is certain

To Inherit the Earth

First, learn to stand.
If bent and broken, allow
a blue sky autumn breeze

through one vertebrae and then another,
until the spine lifts,
a strand of pearls pulled straight
by the hand of God.

If no longer bent,
but still cracked open with hip bones
shattered into a tableau of what should

never happen—then knit.
Knit the bones. Knit together shards
and pieces until the pelvic girdle

is one piece. Whole.
This will require knitting needles heated
on the sun's corona and wool woven

from your mother's womb.
If still unable to stand
since shin bones have split

and cannot carry
the weight of days and nights
bitterly cold
when mylar blankets were not enough,

then crawl, move forward
by grabbing a table leg, the end of a couch,
pull yourself up so you can

at least sit. For a moment. On the front stoop.
Quit smoking and watch a stranger
walk by. Notice the possum asleep

on a gate, the squirrel beginning
to laugh, a piece of broken glass
on the sidewalk caught in midday rays.

Look up,
see leaves on a tree silently
green.

The Bones

The first little piggie went to market
and got stuck on an earring.

The next little piggie
got caught in her hair.

The third and fourth hungry little piggies
chewed down to the bone.

The last little piggie had none.
He cried, *Mee, mee, mee*

until all his five
fingers found a home.

The hand that slaps the face
contains 27 bones, 48 nerves.

Nerves remember as they jump,
shout, turn about.

On a skull, there are holes.
Eye sockets. Nasal passages.

Little holes where ears used to be,
where ants dance. Until we're all bone,

there is no rest. We may
as well be marionettes

stomping drunk on countertops.
How many times

will a metronome beat
before it's all over?

On her cheek. A red imprint.
A hand print. The nerves. The bones.

On your sister's cheek.
On your neighbor's cheek.

On the cheek of the girl across the street.
We, we, we, they cry all the way home.

Ghost Ranch, Abiquiú, New Mexico

Sun-bleached bones were most wonderful against the blue
—Georgia O'Keeffe

    1.   The Library

O'Keeffe's books rest on an oak table. There are bones
everywhere. Dry white bones over a stone floor.

Look at this. Amazing. I will find it. He lost the page
where O'Keeffe drips pelvises the shade of stone floors.

Bleached bones echo what once was. A woman's orange hip.
La Mujer. La Madre. Too many have slept cold on stone floors.

The real question needs a vodka martini to wash down.
Could it have been different? On a bed above a stone floor

in the dark, she became una puta. Octopus ink spreads
a tattoo over a belly button. Scorched stone floors.

Everywhere sex: the hip rise of a mesa range,
the solar flare. All this noise above a stone floor.

On a good day, a bird rotates past. Its azure wing
quietly sends shadow beats across stone floors.

    2.   The Remains

Everywhere. Dry white bones.
Next to the library. O'Keeffe drips pelvises.
A skull casts shadows on a burnt sienna adobe wall.

It's not death, but the remains. Peculiar details
flash back. The tightness, the lack of breath,
the inability to start over—linger. An apprehension

that requires a vodka martini to quiet.
Death does not arrive to quell
the torn and bruised,

only emptiness.

Skulls float. Horns scratch.
Blue sky burns a salty sun.

    3.   She Knows

The mountain curves like a woman

on her knees wiping clean a stone floor.
She looks up. Her reflection
twisted in a transparent sliding glass door.

She is an apparition. She is lost
to herself. The door. A simple slide lock.
She can leave. Step outside. She pauses.

It is possible to flip open the lock.
A car crunches gravel on the driveway.
She hears footsteps. The buzzing heat.

Antlers. Horns. The curve into sky.

    4.   A Martini

At dawn, the desert hums.

The path covered in dirt.
Pebbles scattered
        under
        dry desert mesquite.

A bull's skull ornamentally hung

> over an open doorway.
> Bleached bones white. It is difficult.
> Ask

any mujer who has found herself degraded
on a bed over a stone floor.

Sometimes it gets bad.

Since learning this,
I've needed to sleep
two hours
each afternoon.

Often, I wake

tangled in shadow,

disoriented, angry, ranting, needing a vodka martini.

Jungian Songs and Pastoral Landscapes

for Maggie Paul and Lisa Simon

She loved him. The teacher
who taught her Jungian well-versed manners. He knew
about wailing walls and prayers that sing
sweet honey into rocks. His fingers
played her innocent red ribbons.

A woman can walk barefoot
despite age and sharp pebble pathways.
Living as neighbors for years, she remains
afraid. He might take her, harm her.

The unidentified stranger.

He leers and laughs through Hoboken, New Jersey.
She runs. Then runs again.

She can't stop running
through earth, elemental
dry dust on her toes.

She has pretty legs. A pretty bird.
Bird in a cage. Here pretty bird, *Sing it!*

More unidentified strangers.
They catch a girl.
Put her in a truck. A girl is not
meant to be hunted.

A girl is not a wild animal
to be caught. Her hat should not
tear off and tumble
past a cactus scratching air.

Hats should levitate
on warm whispering winds
to be found by those lost
seeking shade and water.

If you find one
rolling over sand and boulders,
put it on.

Enter an ice blue pool. Float
on an inflatable aqua lounge.

Adjust your sunglasses.

Be grateful. You have found
cool water in the desert while sipping
from a glass of stones.

On Writing

A poem may contain
      a cliff over a sea,

a sea that sharpens a granite edge raw,
        exhales brisk breezes,
        maroons seaweed on beaches,

        breaks shells to cut our feet.

The same sea may slide in softly,
      leave white foam on sand.

The warm sand. The day
           hot enough.

Once I sat in a restaurant without words, and Jorge said
to go outside. Feel the heat. It was necessary

to burn my heavy bones into clear sky,

      to break free from fog,

      that fog that rises
      after a hot day turns
      water into air.

I walked along the shoreline
      the hard sand,
         the cool water,

      and rested in a wilted garden.

In this garden, it is always morning.
A hydrangea moist and blue.

The leaf of a lemon tree rests, fixed and waxy,

next to a sturdy white bud,
a flower yet to come.

Here, when a bee stings, the pain collapses

into pleasure. Because it is over.
Because I have not become numb.

Desert Variation in Blue

if the scar on the mountain
                  is as beautiful as the mountain
let the mountain heal the scar

the mountain rises from desert
                  when seen from a gaseous giant star
the mountain lays down flat

both is and is not
the mountain   the scar

scars rise from broken hands
                  when hands break   God laments

when God rises from broken hands
                  flowers burn iridescent

let the scar heal
       the mountain
       the hand
       God's lament

if the scar on the mountain
                  is as beautiful as the mountain
let the scar heal the mountain

let the scar bring forth
       twilight orange
       cottonwood ethereal plumes
       a yellow desert flower

we are the ones who heal
                  when we see the mountain move

we are the ones who heal

        when we see that the mountain
        cannot move

both is and is not
the mountain   the scar

both heal and do not
the mountain   the scar

we know but we cannot
both is and is not

Desert Variation in Blue II

when the mountain becomes a scar

she rises from the Earth's crust
       tectonic plates   lava plumes   relentless
              fire and steam

we are the ones who see

       where Piñon pines dig deep
       a mountain and her shadows
       even stars that burn holograms in sky

       Orion's bow
       his arrow

       then the wound

and so it is done
       that quickly
       the scar becomes a woman's hip

all that cannot be said
       contained within
       becomes a mountain

she rises in anger
       becomes
       a stick   a stone
       blade or fist

under a nighttime sky
       fog drapes through clawing branches
       broken   torn

       She is alone

Desert Variation in Blue III

heat waves bind desert green on the valley floor
        bluestem   sagebrush   saltbush

we are the ones who see
we are the ones who know

light waves undulate at precise peaks and valleys
we name these   burnt sienna   azure blue   clay white   alabaster

we are the ones who see
we are the ones who know

on the valley floor   she rises
casts shadows that undulate with the passing sun

she is mountain   she is scar   she is bird or star
she sits on a fence

    a bird in shade under a tree
    a bird splashes wet
    a hummingbird over sugary sweet water

in the beginning was the word
    and we began to name   plant   animal   color   star
but that was not enough

A word is and is not
    a nest   a seed   a root that digs deep

she sits in the form of herself
and teeters precariously on the edge of the world

    as a bird on a fence
    as an orange desert flower
    as a giant gaseous star

words lift in wind
    and like leaves on a tree
    she catches afternoon light

Three Variations Near a Mountain

So do not be afraid; you are worth more than many sparrows.
—Matthew 10:31 (NAB)

I.

I have grown Phoenix feathers
                across my shoulder blades, elbows,
        wrists. Arms open. Flowing midair.
                I soar through broken mornings.

Ants scatter on bathroom tiles. Earthworms roil in rain-soaked dirt.

        To die numerous times
but never die. A hand can slap a face, a hand can clench a hammer,
                a hand can break
windows, shrines, bones.

Death becomes our fragile bodies.
Juanita's fingers wrapped round a crucifix. She was no more
                of this world.

        She became clear wind-swept sky.

II.

All this business
of keeping the body warm.

        The you and the I.
Prayers answered by prickly pear cactus in bloom.

The quiet breath of knowing
        a cool adobe wall under a desert moon.

These fingers rustle pearly sands, grasp open doors, radiate other:
        other than despair, other than we're dead.

The rough texture of a Piñon pine.
The sharp point of needle. A drop of blood
smeared dry.

Fingers pluck guitar strings.
Notes rise.
We open to praiseworthy song.

III.

Leaving. Leaving my car in the parking lot. Leaving a lion in a cage, a spider in a web, a shark in a cold sea. Leaving, leaving behind. It was through my hands, my fingers, the skin and bones, I became the Piñon pine, the pearly sand. My mother held me close. She lifted me into this life. At sunrise, she manifests near a mountain. May love continue. En tiempos buenos y en tiempos malos. Say yes. Nestle down slow para siempre. Juanita. My mother. Her fingers never let go. She rose into the sky, only to stay. A bird lands on a branch. Shakes loose a hillside. A wisp of cloud. All that we need.

III

The art of losing isn't hard to master;
so many things seem filled with the intent
to be lost that their loss is no disaster.

—Elizabeth Bishop from "One Art"

What Changed

After I changed one husband for another,

       I changed my shoes.
       I changed my earrings.
       My dreams changed, too.

       I began slamming doors
       and shouting—*No!*

       A blue Cadillac crashed
       while driving Camino Real.

            The only part that stayed
            were words
            that swam in cool ocean water.

After I changed one husband for another,

       I cast a spell in a dream.
       I changed my shoes.
       I changed my earrings.
          I changed the locks,
       the bedspread, sheets, and towels.

       Sadness and loss
       changed to dancing
       a cha-cha two step

       under a moon and a star.

       I began walking
          a mountain trail filled
          with eucalyptus and blue jays.

After changing one husband for another,

       I heard a moon and a star
       laugh in a twilight sky.
       I changed my shoes.
       I changed my earrings.
            I changed the locks,

       clouds fanned toward mountains,
       rain fell onto asphalt,
       and leaves stuck wet

       like a sentence that has too many
       participles and lacks
       concrete nouns.

After changing one husband for another

       I changed my shoes.
       I changed my earrings.
       I changed the words.
       The weather changed
       from autumn to winter

       and I learned to rest
       my head on a shoulder.

       I heard a moon and a star
       laugh in a twilight sky.
       I cast a spell, so the words
       that swam in deep waters

       could seep out from wounds

       as letters
       rising into space.

When a Poem Falls from Heaven

When a poem falls from heaven,
        gallons of milk and loaves of bread
        expire at the corner market,

        the past due electric bill
        slides into the mailbox,

        and the stainless steel pot
        from last night's dinner
        remains on the stove.

When a poem falls from heaven,
        fish with antennae
        project light in the deep sea,

        my father and abuelita float
        to the stars
        in the embers from a burning log,

        pericos perch
        in rainforest canopies.

When a poem falls from heaven,
        fog on the bay rests like memories
        of the homeland, platanos fritos y queso.
        And yes, sweet is good.

        I can write on the margins
        of a loose-leaf notebook,

        pick hermit crabs off the beach
        in San Juan del Sur,
        slip a sailboat into a bottle,
        flip three tortillas on a comal.

When a poem falls from heaven,
    words repeat on billboards, in headlines,
    across cinder block walls.

    They rise from a cup's broken handle,
    a window pane's cracked frame,
    a hand mirror's shattered glass,

    and from leaves as they crumble
    and birds fly north.

When a poem falls from heaven,
    hombres, mujeres, the gendered not,
    speak the world.

    My car speeds through a yellow light
    at the corner of the moon and Saturn.

    Waves slide over sand crabs
    while flames turn into coal
    low and warm on a beach campfire.

When a poem falls from heaven,
    I listen to my mother's phrases,
    her vowels cry in my ear;
    it is necessary to hear her life
    as she blinks, smiles, turns
    a ring on her finger.

    Let us focus on the words
    from my mother's lips:
    Mi'ja. Ven aca.
    My mother never kissed me, will you?

What Poetry Told Me

The week Poetry stayed at my house,
she kept a razor in a wooden box. Poetry
refused to abandon her ancestors
and paid homage to the octagonal black
tourmaline rising up from underneath
the burden of boulders. She joined in song
with La Virgen and burned down the barriers between us.
She was interested in rhyme and the metaphorical.
Her rhythm shattered glass, but she did not finish
what she began to carve into stone. She was fickle.
First she drank mead, then preferred a martini.
Poetry wore a new necklace every day. Still,
she prayed for us. Words as omens and talismans.
But she couldn't really do anything. She never
made dinner or even brewed coffee.
She was horrible at baking.
Soon enough, Poetry abandoned everything,
left flour all over the counters,
the dough proofing unbaked in the oven.
On her way to the airport,
she texted one last entreaty,
something about an old oak tree
unfurling leaves, glossy and new
but with sharpened points
that can make a poet bleed.

When Poetry Arrived After Reading Neruda

I don't know where it comes from,
the sin of loving too much and too freely.
I was born through a rush of blood
and water into a fresh howling scream.
There were no words,
yet there was no silence.
Poetry arrived in shadow,
in the scent of a pillow case,
in sheets of rain outside a window.
I was wearing my mother's face
and my father's indifference.
I learned how shame sews lips shut
and to listen to vowels primed
under a tropical sun,
a Spanish lilt to English vowels.
A,E,I,O,U. El burro sabe más que tú.

With a woman's sin come words
that cannot carry. At first,
I began with a rhythmic gait
that threw knives and shattered
guitars. Then, I began to write
what lies North, then South, and now, here,
a Stellar Jay and his bright blue body
hopping up cast iron stairs.
I don't know what it means,
but I am getting used to the taste
of multicolored pebbles
and to the sound of snail shells,
cracked and dried yellow. I tell
the boys, *Enough now. It is time*
to think about other things.

When poetry arrived,
she unwrapped fingers
clenched around my throat
and broke the silence
of my mother's sins.

Volcanic Poetics

After iguanas ran off with the sun,
after pericos emerged violently squawking,

after soldiers left
bullet holes and torn mattresses

and the dictator collected
music boxes and skulls,

a song rose from the stink
of a river festering yellow mud

where one eye of a crocodile
watched you, I, we, todos

break bones, break bodies.
I want to tell you about after,

how bones knit, courage rises,
and we stave off despair.

Once in that country filled with mango trees,
where sharks live in fresh water,

where monkeys are kept on leashes,
where the ice cream is salty,

el ministerio de Cultura issued
a call to language

as action, a call to write poems
about ordinary objects

and Exteriorismo began stirring
a pot of beans, adding

oil and then leftover rice,
to make gallo pinto. A plain dish

that Danny likes, a child, our child,
here in the States with Nica blood.

Poems are his legacy,
along with a lava-filled past

that percolated a revolution
of sound, vida, y ranas,

ranitas, little froggies on a farm
on the road to Momotombo.

My mother's words
explode volcanic vowels.

¡Ay! ¡Cómo queman!
The slow burn down

the side of a mountain
with its top blown off.

Nature on fire. Poetry
a living thing.

En la voz de Abuelita 'Minta

The sin is sex. We all give in.
Especially, if we're pretty.
If we're young. If we're married
to un sinvergüenza.
Have babies. That's
what we're supposed to do.
Rezar a los santos. La virgen.
Papaje'us. San Martín
con su escoba y perritos. Hope
it all turns out. But you're not
supposed to like it. Yes. I did.
And then the babies.
I had eight. One right after the other.
Six boys, the last two girls. M'ijos.
Mine. And they did what I told them.
We had to stick together.
Who else was going to take care of us?
Juanita's babies slept
in my bed under a brown satin
comforter. I tried to tell her
to keep her legs closed. To barter
that beauty for something
that stays. The little one, Adelita,
está bonita, like her mother.
Esos labios y carita linda.
Trouble is coming. Again.

En la voz de mi madre

What Lola wants, Lola gets. Once
I stole onto a train and rode all the way
to León. By myself. I was fourteen.
I wanted to leave ese Tío
malvado and be with my brothers.
But they sent me back. I didn't stay long.
My first job was smiling.
I was a receptionist behind a counter.
I knew how to work,
but they didn't pay enough.
A Pan Am flight me llamaba
a los Estados Unidos.
San Francisco. LA. Downey.
My kids. My job. My money
that I earned. My house
that I bought. Oh, see what I have seen.
Oh, taste what I have tasted.
We all have our secrets. I don't regret
a thing. I hang a picture of Papachú
above the TV. Our souls
in the hands of the Father. No nos dejes
caer en tentación y líbranos del mal.
I still say it in Spanish
even though it's been over sixty years.
Stepping on las playas de Poneloya
my shoulders burned. Freckles
cover my back like a shawl of stars.

En la voz de mi padre

Morning arrives. Coffee, then something
sweet. Sometimes the sweat of a woman.
Sometimes pan dulce. Sometimes chasing tail
of a good deal. A bathroom to remodel.
A kitchen floor to lay. Esa mujer that still
looks good in a bikini. Sí, yo soy
mujeriego. Every flower blooms bright.
I'm a good father. Soy buena gente. My father
didn't even know who I was. I know
all my children. And their mothers.
Even the one who doesn't know he is mine.
He's got the same dimpled chin. I saw him
dancing at a wedding. He looked just like me.
I waited. I waited for them all to call. Adelita
asked, *Do you want me to call a priest?* ¿Para qué?
Yo no creo en eso. Then breath stopped.
Startled. The one molecule of me broke down
into air, space, to time without sweat.
The breeze. Outside. There was a tree.
I moved leaves. I rose into cloud. Then
the weight of water. Heavy. I fell as rain.

The Beauty Contest

At nine years old I wanted
fat shiny knees like my grandmother's.
They glistened soft and smooth,
love arising iridescent from skin.

When my mother was nine,
that same grandmother took
the back of a hair brush
and welted her little girl legs.

There has always been a soft whispering
between my mother and me.

My seeking and her giving.
We both know what it is to want
and how from that you end up

tending feral cats residing
behind Burger King.
One blinded by a dull branch,
another born without a diaphragm, weakly
breathing. She saved them both

and paid good money to a vet.

When my mother was nine she lived
in the humid heat of Managua.
She was always hungry and wanted
one pearl looped through a necklace.

When I was nine I lived at the bottom of the stairs
outside our apartment in Pico Rivera.
I wanted my mother.

She always came home late, the TV still on.
She'd heat up leftovers,
tell me stories. Nicaragua. Long ago.

Her mother. Her brothers. My Tío Ernesto.

Once at the edge of the Pacific, she stood
on Ernesto's shoulders and prepared to dive
into a warm sea, as if hoping to win a tiara
in a beauty contest.

Nothing like that was forthcoming.

The sea had turned away.
She landed sideways on sand.
Her collarbone broken.

After Years in the States

Managua lingers in the kitchen
like the smell of an overripe orange
at the bottom of a fruit bowl.
My mother sits at a table.

Then gets up. Creaky fingers
pour kibble into a cat bowl.

Mami—why didn't you ever go back?

> *We all went away from the sun.*
> *The water was too salty and the crustaceans*
> *died. Flames flickered in the Masaya crater*
> *but we couldn't climb the steep slope.*
>
> *They looked under our beds and in closets.*
> *They found nothing. Took everything.*
>
> *M'ija—What was there to go back for?*
> *Spanish sticks to the roof of my mouth*
> *and a perico's tongue squawks too loud.*

With Ash on Their Wings

I carry sulfuric fog. I carry atmosphere.
I carry a bottle of Flor de Caña, rosquillas,
and a steaming volcanic caldera.
I carry memories of when he held my hand.
He is a glass of lemonade that needs more sugar.
I carry Papi inside.
We would walk around the corner
to Mitchell's ice cream shop.
He would let me order whatever I wanted
and listened to my little girl chatter.
After we got home,
I would hear the front door open, again.
Then close. As he left,
my father would skip down the stairs,
whistling a happy tune.
He skis down a mountain in my dreams
and smiles through a moustache.
I tell him the condo next door
has nearly doubled in value
and we have bounced back
from the recession. I carry his ambition.
I carry his broken tongue.
I carry mangoes, nacatamales, y pinolillo.
I don't have his straight black hair,
but I share that wink in his eye.
He is all right. He has been forgiven.
When did I do that?
Hey, Papi. Does the sand from Cerro Negro burn?
Can parrots fly with ash on their wings?
It would have been nice to salsa
with him at my cousin's pachanga
but instead I foxtrotted with a man
who couldn't pronounce my name.

El Perico Verde

My father grew up under a verdant jungle sky.
He listened to el perico verde de Nicaragua.
She always told him what he had done wrong.
My father chewed limes with salt. He knew bitter times.

He listened to el perico verde de Nicaragua and ignored
what he had done wrong. He sliced olives into arroz con pollo
and chewed limes with salt. He knew bitter times.
He never bit a red apple, only los jocotes presented by Eve.

My father sliced olives and all he did wrong into arroz con pollo.
Eve smiled before turning off the light on the nightstand.
He never bit a red apple, only los jocotes presented by Eve.
My father was grassy green lust that loved platanos fritos.

Eve smiled before turning off the light on the nightstand.
The perico verde told him he was wrong. My father ignored
that silly bird. He was grassy green lust that loved platanos fritos.
My father stole all the limes, olives, avocadoes and apples.

The perico verde told him he was wrong. My father ignored
that silly bird. He became a broken couch, old from too much wear.
My father stole all the limes, olives, avocadoes and apples.
He wore a bathrobe over a V-neck T-shirt. Pajama bottom pants.

Ignoring that silly bird, he became a broken couch, old.
Eve no longer wore a nightgown in his bed or tempted him
with jocotes. My father tied a bathrobe sash around his old man waist.
On his feet were worn brown leather slippers.

Eve no longer wore a nightgown in his bed or tempted him
with jocotes. One windy afternoon, he faded into a light green rain.
On his feet were worn brown leather slippers.
My father grew up under a verdant jungle sky.

Los volcánes de Nicaragua

for my father

Cosigüina: North

North only North—no trails, steep slopes.
Stand at the rim of the crater,
pour your mother out:

The mother who left you in Managua.
The mother who brought you to the States.

San Cristóbal Volcano: Travel

St. Christopher is not a saint
but a martyr   protects nevertheless.

Planes and visas take so many North,
then REVOLUCIÓN:
trucks lined with palm fronds,
everyone celebrates.

Cerro Negro Volcano: Hills

Except you.   You liked Somoza, the dictator,
the special contracts, the ability
to sit in a hotel,
order a steak with red wine reduction,
mushrooms in a cream sauce.

Did you sand board down the slope
of an active volcano?

El Hoyo: Emptiness

If your mother leaves
and doesn't come back,
are you left on the edge of a volcano?
Will you keep jumping into lava

to burn away the loss?
Will love feel like heat
for the rest of your life?

Momotombo: Energy

Managua with its geothermal plant
at the base of a volcano
is like a woman undressing
for the first time.

The city simmers hot.
So many women.
So many times.

Apoyeque: Sulfur

Volcanoes in a chain
are like generations

one after the other
that keep doing
the same thing:

combustion, volatile gases,
the tremble of tectonic plates crashing.

Except, I mean bodies
with other bodies.

Except, I mean feeding
the body with other bodies

until there is

only ash.

Volcanic Heat

With a lava lake roiling below, my mother
stood at the rim of a volcano. She knew

it was not too late. She sold a golden crucifix,
said goodbye to her brothers, packed

a medicine bottle with pulverized obsidian sand.
The volcano inside her was quiet. She was calm.

The volcano wasn't something she could lose.
It would always be with her. When my father

became a letter, my mother ate a wedding cake
that that no one could see. She became

an unstoppable force. My mother
turned up the music and began to dance.

She curtailed the gossip, then heated
a knife with magma flames to sever

the umbilical cords of my brother and I.
With the volcano's heat inside her, she had children

outside of marriage. My mother changed the landscape.
Molten bombs shot into sky. Seismic booms rattled.

Fire rocks avalanched down. Lava flowed.
Ash dusted sidewalks with poltergeists

and premonitions of coming revolutions. She continued
to create possibility by curling hair and setting rollers.

My mother did the impossible: in her old age,
with the heat and rage of the volcano

capped tight by cooled solid rock, she laughed
as a cat chased my father's ghost up a tree.

Chantico Swings

She doesn't speak German, English
or Spanish. She is prior to the four directions,
prior to Sandino, Somoza, US Marines, AK-47s,
cocaine, and communists.

She is queen of the underworld
inside the Masaya crater.
After bathing in the fires of a lava lake,
she dances on red hot boulders.

When she drinks foaming elixirs,
séance tables rise and tambourines
sound the failed heartbeats of the dead.

Sometimes when the dead are too chatty,
she opens a bottle of Flor de Caña so that all
will have breath sweetened with rum.

Before Pan Am flights out of Managua
landed in San Francisco,
Chantico was one of many girls.
Then she trembled and the plaster wall
joining her bedroom to the kitchen
cracked, bricks tumbled.

She was a woman now.
After a swill of methane, she exhales
like Marlene Dietrich.
Only smoke remains.

Chantico Flames

When looking up saints and goddesses
that crackle through soil
in a homeland I've only seen once,

I found Chantico Inn & Suites, Chantico Global,
Chantico Fire, corporate fumes
smoldering from the goddess,
her home, hearth, and volcanic royal

menstrual blood. Chiconahui Itzcuintli
sent warriors into battle who prayed
she would bathe their hearts in fire.

No longer. Chantico, simply a name
for a Starbucks six ounce chocolate drink
with a pinch of cayenne. Her heat, her fire,
flows through every woman's veins.

We bleed lava lakes. We are Gaia.
But not strong enough to melt conquistador helmets,
chainmail, and swords.

The Telica eruption couldn't take out Somoza's eldest son.
He kept riding a stallion through black lava sand.
Girls hiding blood stains on panties
stopped speaking as parrots mocked
them from treetops.

My mother didn't marry Reynoldo or build
a mini-mall with a hair salon,
fashion emporium, and an agua frescas quick stop.

My mother came here. Learned English. Sent me
to college. Chola? Cholita? Chiconahui,
Chicona, Chingona? Now Chantico turns up

in different cities spouting flames as she speaks
lilting Spanish vowels. With ruby lips, she stacks

paper bags into a red Ford Fiesta.

Below the Momotombo Volcano

Whenever the gods and goddesses of volcanoes meet up for a barbeque, they gather at Chantico's place. Her fat iron wood stove breathes fire. The first to show up are always the dwarfs and giants. They rise out of Icelandic snow with a tremble and shake, then lug in coolers filled with vodka shooters. Hephaestus is a little late. He brings the tea set and silverware having turned rage into art in his studio at a prominent address on Piccadilly Square. Heph is still steaming after being conceived by pure female juju and thrown off a cliff. He went free-falling for 24 hours. Even though he landed on his feet, he never could walk right. Out back by the cascading red flowers of the banana trees, Vulcan sets up Tiki torches to keep away the buzz. There's a Twitter feed on him about complicity in forging lances for conquistadores, Remington rifles for US Yankee banana companies, and AK-47s for the School of the Americas. It's rumored he had a hand in welding jeeps, grenades, high speed bullets, and landmines for Somoza. He did the same for the Sandinistas, the same for the Contras, the same for this army, for that army. Vulcan doesn't discriminate. Anywhere heat is needed to forge a cause of destruction, he's willing to oblige. He's so long winded and never gets to the point that in order to cope, Mt. St. Helens begins to layer charcoal while Pele pulls out a Zippo lighter. The women spark an idea while tending the barbeque smoke and flames. Why not create a train of volcanoes so that each child born on Central American soil will carry the power of fire in their left pinky? It can begin with a mother drying corn. After she ascends the slopes of Momotombo for flame to heat el comal, a freckle will be born of fire and from then on all children of the Americas will carry an affinity for the left and all that burns.

Looking Under Tombstones on Día de los Muertos

My ancestors are women without men.
        The men drank themselves into shivering skeletons.

My ancestors are women without men.
        The men ran away into other lives,
        only to drink themselves hollow.

My ancestors are women without men.
        The men did not know what to do
        with these creatures that brought life to sons and daughters,
        so they began mixing whiskey with honey laced water.

My ancestors are women without men.
        The men desired bosoms, tender hearts, tight hips,
        but couldn't stay with the pulsing psychic connection
        emitted from a vagina in love,
        so they opened dusty bottles of 40 proof liquor.

My ancestors are women without men
        because the men were overwhelmed
        by the power of vaginas, amplified breasts,
        and the ecstatic visage of a woman in love at the height of orgasm.
        They began to drink, then run, from one caldera to the next
        dodging the ballistic boulders sent shooting across sky by goddesses.

My ancestors are women
who stand at the rim of volcanoes
and issue forth magma fountains.
They ignite air, sea, land, and sky
into lightning, thunder, tornadoes, and hurricanes.

Before the Volcano Blows

I will speak Spanish
to many stray dogs with fleas
and find my way

to a nameless street
where angels spoke
to my mother as a girl.

Momotombo will simmer
its volatile breath
rumbling and roaring
in the background.

It will be a simple matter,
by then,
to stand at the edge
of a world percolating
madness and volcanic tears.

All the secrets
will have been released
in an ash plume,
smoky and hot,
dusting the rainforest canopy
between Managua and León.

The few vowels left
will explode from parrots squawking
and truth will rain down
upon the poor and tired
scratching their endless memories.

This is all because of my mother,
born on a finca far away
from town. It took days to register
she had broken into the world
wailing a cacophony of lament.

I can never recall her exact birthday.
Was it on the 22nd or the 28th
that she began the legacy
of keeping secrets, gold hoop

earrings looping through
pain and dispossession?

Too many have withstood
the cataclysm of broken doors,
the harangue of voices
that never cease, the visceral scars
on bodies that know too much
of what has come before.

When I finally arrive
with my own broken being
packed tight
in a worn leather bag,

I will not cry into satin blankets.

Instead, I will sip mint tea
with two ice cubes slowly melting
as my hair curls
into ash and dust.

After the Volcano Ate the Moon

It was dark. The bike did not have reflectors.
I did not have a helmet. I went anyway.

When I approached a car pulling out of a driveway
with a—*Hey, Hey, I'm here. I'm here,*
a man in an Audi scolded me. He said I should
get a light. I didn't like his tone of voice,

so the volcano ate him. I was doing good.

I had cleared the road and was on the bike path.
The trail was smooth and divided
by a yellow line. I stayed on my side.

The meadow was to my right.
Dwarf pines rippled in wind.
Since I thought the trees were pretty,
right after I rode past their quivering,

the volcano ate them.

She was jealous—our heart chakras
pulse the same beat. She's always insisting
on my undivided attention.

I was riding fast, wind massaging my hair,
and still I thought the moon would arrive
at any moment. I didn't hit a stray rock and fall.

The volcano had eaten them all.

I stayed on the trail and passed two women with a dog
and another woman jogging,
music seeping out from headphones.

When the dog barked at the nonexistent moon,
the volcano ate it.

Then she ate the women. She has been impossible
to control.

The volcano has an indiscriminate palate.
She keeps many secrets to herself.

I noticed stars lit the night sky.
A deep blue stillness arose
from the mountain.

I began to think about the volcano,
about how rocks within rocks
melt down to magma.

All the rumble and rage.
How heat and passion
flow down a mountainside.

The beauty of glass formed
as a volcano weeps, then
the dry edge of volcanic rock.

Each time, the sky thunders,
a suffocating ash.

I stopped for a moment.
The sky blushed dark navy and stars.

I remembered—
the volcano and I are one.

Careful. We burn red hot.

Acknowledgments

The poems in this collection were written with the support of many literary organizations, fellow poets, and friends. I am deeply grateful for your support, kindness, and belief in my work. It is through community that we flourish.

The ekphrastic poems in this collection arose during the *Pintura: Palabra* workshops held in conjunction with the Smithsonian American Art Museum's "Our America: The Latino in Presence in American Art" exhibit that toured the US. Thank you, Francisco Aragón, and Letras Latinas, the literary initiative at the University of Notre Dame's Institute for Latino Studies, for inviting me to the Crocker Museum in Sacramento, where I wrote the first drafts of numerous ekphrastic poems. In addition, I would like to thank Francisco for all his support over the years and for his sage advice and mentoring. Thank you, Francisco, for all that you do to promote Latine/x literature.

I am also indebted to Cristina García and her Dos Brujas conferences in Abiquiú, New Mexico, and the San Francisco Mission. The desert landscapes and fractured scars on the mountain that appear in these poems arise from the Abiquiú landscape and through a workshop with Juan Felipe Herrera. Thank you both, Cristina and Juan Felipe, for the inspiration to break language into its crumbling parts that, when forged together, form something new.

I want to thank Ellen Bass for the inspiration to dig deep and write about trauma through numerous workshops over the years. Thank you, Ellen, for creating safe spaces where writers can explore how language can heal the deepest wounds.

The volcanic poems in this collection were started at a summer poetry workshop held by the Community of Writers at Olympic Valley. Thank you, comadres y compadres, who were there and witnessed the beginning of the lava flows.

I am indebted to my writing groups, the Emerald Street Poets and ERA, for reading the first drafts of the poems in this collection. Your insights and suggestions always guide me to elevate my work to the next level. Thank you for welcoming me into loving and safe spaces where I can share the most intimate of all endeavors—writing from the truth of my bilingual-bicultural experience. Thanks to Marcia Adams, Len Anderson, Dane Cervine, Andrew Fague, Robin Lysne, Joanna Martin, Tom McCoy, Margaret Paul, Stuart Presley, Lisa Simon, Robin Straub, Janet Trenchard, and Philip Wagner (Emerald Street Poets), and Erin Redfern and Renée Schell (ERA).

I want to thank Nikia Chaney at Jamii Press for her friendship, inspiration, and for publishing *Volcanic Interruptions*, a chapbook that includes Janet Trenchard's paintings and selected poems in this collection. Thank you, Nikia, for seeing the beauty of Janet's paintings and how the volcanic heat from my family's Nicaraguan history could percolate on the page. Thank you, Janet, for collaborating with me during the pandemic and connecting your visual art to my poems.

Over the years, Círculo de poetas and Writers has fortified my mission to write and share my vision of being an activist writer. Through a círculo of connection, we have created community where the Latine/x voice is welcomed, nourished, and celebrated. It has been a pleasure to commune with all of you and listen to the vast complexity of the Latine/x experience. Thank you to Paul Aponte, Lucha Corpi, Odilia Galván Rodríguez, Arnoldo García, Javier O. Huerta, Aideed Medina, Violeta Orozco, Naomi Quiñonez, and to all participants over the years with whom I have had the pleasure of meeting and living the literary life.

I would also like to thank Cabrillo College and the Puente Project for supporting my work as a writer/educator serving our Latine/x students at the community colleges in California. Through Cabrillo and Puente, I have met many like-minded writers/educators who have become a lively and supportive network. I thank you all, and may the work continue!

The editorial suggestions from Shanna McNair and Scott Wolven, directors and editors at The Writer's Hotel, were indispensable as I completed the final version of this collection. Thank you so much for your editorial eye, candor, and steadfast support.

Finally, Gregory Wendell McNair, my husband, is at the heart of these poems. Your unwavering support and love have nurtured me to find the courage and strength to complete this collection. Your steadfast presence in my life allows me to grow and reach for the impossible. Gregorovich, I am so grateful to have built this life together with you.

I wish to thank the editors and publications where versions of these poems first appeared:
"What Poetry Told Me" appeared in *Poetry*, 2024.

"Again, Nicaragua" and "The Parking Lot" appeared in *Huizache*, 2024.

"On Viewing Gronk's *Illegal Landscape / Paisaje Ilegal*" appeared in *About Place Journal–Strange Wests* edition, 2024.

"To Inherit the Earth" appeared in *Xinachtli Journal–Journal X*, 2023.

"With Ash on Their Wings" appeared as "Mi Papi" in the national edition of *Red Wheelbarrow*, 2023.

"Poneloya Poolside Party" appeared in the *Catamaran Literary Reader*, 2023.

"After the Volanco Ate the Moon," "Before the Volcano Blows," "Below the Momotombo Volcano," "Chantico Flames," "Chantico Swings," "Looking Under Tombstones . . .," "Los Volcánes de Nicaragua," and "Volcanic Poetics" appear in the chapbook *Volcanic Interruptions*, Jamii Press, 2023.

"After the Volcano Ate the Moon" appeared in the *Porter Gulch Review*, 2022.

"The Bones" appeared in *Tule Review*, 2021.

"Ghost Ranch, Abiquiú, New Mexico" was originally a three-poem series; "The Library" appeared as "A Martini Over a Stone Floor" in *Plainsongs*, 2020, while parts two and three appeared as "A Stone Floor" and "Another Stone Floor" in *The Dollhouse on High Literary Journal*, 2020.

"Los volcánes de Nicaragua" and "En la voz de mi padre" appeard in *Anacua Literary Arts Journal ~ Migrations*, 2019.

"The History of Food," "The History of Food II," "The History of Food III" appeared in *Crab Orchard Review*, 2019.

"Volcanic Heat" appeared in *The Account*, 2019.

"Chantico Swings" appeared in *Nimrod International Journal*, 2018.

"Barbecue below the Momotombo Volcano" appeared as as "What Happened at the Barbecue below the Momotombo Volcano," *Catamaran Literary Reader* (2018), as well as "On Writing."

"La Virgen de las Patadas" appeared in the *Packinghouse Review*, 2017.

"Chantico Flames" appeared as "Los volcánes de Nicaragua." *Written Here: The Community of Writers*, 2016.

"After Years in the States" appeared as "After 60+ Years in the States" in the *Porter Gulch Review*, 2017.

"Iguana Dreams" appeared in the *About Place Journal*, 2016.

"Star Variation in Blue" appeared as "Incantation 2.1" in *phren-Z* , 2013.

"Desert Variation in Blue" appeared as "Incantation One" in the *Acentos Review* 2013, as well as "I Have Heard."

"An Ambiguity" appeared in *BorderSenses*, 2011.

Biographical Note

Adela Najarro serves on the board of directors for Círculo de poetas and Writers and works with the Latine/x community nationwide, promoting the intersection of creative writing and social justice. She is the author of four poetry collections: *Split Geography, Twice Told Over, My Childrens,* and *Volcanic Interruptions,* a chapbook that includes Janet Trenchard's artwork. The 2024 Int'l Latino Book Awards designated *Volcanic Interruptions* as an Honorable Mention in the Juan Felipe Herrera Best Poetry Book Award category. Her extended family left Nicaragua and arrived in San Francisco during the 1940s; after the fall of the Somoza regime, the last of the family settled in the Los Angeles area. The California Arts Council has recognized her as an established artist for the Central California Region and appointed her as an Individual Artist Fellow.

www.ingramcontent.com/pod-product-compliance
Lightning Source LLC
Jackson TN
JSHW080828190125
77340JS00010B/4